SUPER COLOSSAL KNOCK-KNOCKS

Xtra Awesome Laughs

A LITTLE GIANT® BOOK

SUPER COLOSSAL KNOCK-KNOCKS

Xtra Awesome Laughs

Chris Tait & Jacqueline Horsfall

STERLING

New York / London
www.sterlingpublishing.com/kids

Library of Congress Cataloging-in-Publication Data Available

4 6 8 10 9 7 5 3

Published by Sterling Publishing Co., Inc.
387 Park Avenue South, New York, NY 10016

Illustrated by Buck Jones, Mark Zahnd, Rob Collinet, Sanford Hoffman,
Lance Lekander. and Jackie Snider.

Material in this collection was adapted from *Dr. Knucklehead's Knock-
Knocks* (text © by Chris Tait, illustrations by Lance Lekander), *Kids' Silliest
Knock-Knocks* (text © by Jacqueline Horsfall, illustrations by Buck Jones),
Ridiculous Knock-Knocks (text © by Chris Tait, illustrations by Mark
Zahnd), *Funniest Riddle Book in the World* (illustrations by Sanford
Hoffman), *Kids' Silliest Riddles* (illustrations by Buck Jones), *Ridiculous
Riddles* (illustrations by Mark Zahnd), *Kids' Kookiest Riddles* (illustrations
by Rob Collinet), *Joke & Riddle Ballyhoo* (illustrations copyright © by Jackie
Snider), *Kids' Silliest Jokes* (illustrations by Buck Jones), *Super Goofy Jokes*
(illustrations copyright © by Rob Collinet), and *Greatest Goofiest Jokes*
(illustrations by Buck Jones).

Distributed in Canada by Sterling Publishing
c/o Canadian Manda Group, 165 Dufferin Street,
Toronto, Ontario, Canada M6K 3H6
Distributed in the United Kingdom by GMC Distribution Services,
Castle Place, 166 High Street
Lewes, East Sussex, England BN7 1XU
Distributed in Australia by Capricorn Link (Australia) Pty. Ltd.
P.O. Box 704, Windsor, NSW 2756, Australia

Printed in China

Sterling ISBN-13: 978-1-4027-4993-3
ISBN-10: 1-4027-4993-7

For information about custom editions, special sales, premium and
corporate purchases, please contact Sterling Special Sales
Department at 800-805-5489 or specialsales@sterlingpub.com.

contents

A

Knock-knock!
 Who's there?
Aaron.
 Aaron who?
Aaron my tires, gas in my
tank...so let's go!

Knock-knock!
 Who's there?
Ada.
 Ada who?
Ada hamburger, yum-
yum...want one?

Knock-knock!
 Who's there?
Aisle.
 Aisle who?
Aisle never tell your
secret.

Knock-knock!
 Who's there?
Alaska.
 Alaska who?
Alaska, but I don't think
Mom will let me bungee
jump.

Knock-Knock!
 Who's there?
Albee!
 Albee who?
Albee right back, don't
move!

Knock-knock!
 Who's there?
Aleta.
 Aleta who?
Aleta whole pizza by
myself.

Knock-knock!
Who's there?
Alfie!
Alfie who?
Alfie better when you let
me in!

Knock-knock!
Who's there?
Alfred!
Alfred who?
Alfred ever talks about is
fishing!

Knock-Knock!
Who's there?
Ali!
Ali who?
Ali wanna do
is dance!

KNOCK-KNOCK!
Who's there?
Alice!
Alice who?
Alice not lost, my friend!

14

Knock-knock!
 Who's there?
Althea.
 Althea who?
Althea when I get out of
detention.

15

Knock-Knock!
 Who's there?
Alvin!
 Alvin who?
Alvin a nice time on your
porch, since you ask!

Knock-knock!
Who's there?
Amanda!
Amanda who?
Amanda help out around
the house would be nice!

KNOCK-KNOCK!
Who's there?
Amaso!
Amaso who?
Amaso sorry you don't
remember me!

Knock-knock!
 Who's there?
Ammonia.
 Ammonia who?
Ammonia little kid, so I
can't reach the doorbell.

Knock-knock!
 Who's there?
Amos!
 Amos who?
Amos be going; I can't
wait around!

Knock-knock!
 Who's there?
Andrew.
 Andrew who?
Andrew on the walls, and
was her mother mad!

KNOCK-KNOCK!

 Who's there?
Andy!
 Andy who?
Andy body home?

Knock-knock!
 Who's there?
Anemone!
 Anemone who?
Anemone wouldn't knock,
so don't worry!

Knock-Knock!
  Who's there?
Anita!
  Anita who?
Anita another knock-
knock joke like I need a
hole in the head!

21

Knock-Knock!
 Who's there?
Annie!
 Annie who?
Annie thing I can do for
you today?

Knock-Knock!
 Who's there?
Answer!
 Answer who?
Answer all over your porch! It's a mess out here!

Knock-knock!
 Who's there?
Appeal.
 Appeal who?
Appeal is what covers a
banana.

Knock-knock!
 Who's there?
Archibald.
 Archibald who?
Archibald, but he's
buying a wig tomorrow.

KNOCK-KNOCK!

Who's there?
Arnie!
Arnie who?
Arnie ya even gonna
open the door?

Knock-Knock!
Who's there?
Arthur!
Arthur who?
Arthur any other kind of
jokes you know?

Knock-Knock!
 Who's there?
Asia!
 Asia who?
Asia matter of fact, I don't
remember!

KNOCK-KNOCK!
Who's there?
Asp!
Asp who?
Asp me no questions, I'll tell you no lies!

Knock-Knock!
 Who's there?
Astronaut!
 Astronaut who?
Astronaut here, come
back later!

KNOCK-KNOCK!
 Who's there?
Avery!
 Avery who?
Avery time I come to your
house, we go through
this!

Knock-Knock!
 Who's there?
Axel!
 Axel who?
Axel nicely and I might
tell ya!

B

Knock-knock!
 Who's there?
Bacon.
 Bacon who?
Bacon a chocolate cake
for your birthday.

Knock-Knock!
  Who's there?
Bar-B-Q!
  Bar-B-Q who?
Bar-B-Q-t, but I think
you're even cuter!

KNOCK-KNOCK!
  Who's there?
Barked!
  Barked who?
Barked my car in the
middle of the road—
let's go!

Knock-knock!
 Who's there?
Barry.
 Barry who?
Barry rude of you not to
answer the door.

KNOCK-KNOCK!

Who's there?
Bat!
Bat who?
Bat you can't guess!

Knock-knock!
  Who's there?
Bearskin.
  Bearskin who?
Bearskin hibernate in
caves all winter.

Knock-Knock!

Who's there?
Becka!
Becka who?
Becka the bus is the best place to sit!

Knock-knock!
 Who's there?
Bed.
 Bed who?
Bed you can't tell I've got
a code in my nose.

Knock-knock!
 Who's there?
Bee hive!
 Bee hive who?
Bee hive yourself and let
me in!

Knock-knock!
  Who's there?
Beets!
  Beets who?
Beets me—I thought you
might know!

KNOCK-KNOCK!
  Who's there?
Bellows!
  Bellows who?
Bellows me five bucks
and I've come to collect!

Knock-Knock!
 Who's there?
Ben!
 Ben who?
Ben a long time since I've
seen you!

Knock-knock!

Who's there?
Ben Hur.
Ben Hur who?
Ben Hur an hour. Let me in!

Knock-Knock!
 Who's there?
Benny!
 Benny who?
Benny thing happening?

Knock-knock!
 Who's there?
Beth.
 Beth who?
Beth wishes on your
birthday, thweetheart.

Knock-knock!
 Who's there?
Billows!
 Billows who?
Billows me ten bucks and
said you'd give it to me!

Knock-knock!
 Who's there?
Biplane!
 Biplane who?
Biplane or by boat, I told
you I'd come!

Knock-Knock!

Who's there?
Bingo!
Bingo who?
Bingo-ing to this school
long?

Knock-knock!
 Who's there?
Bison!
 Bison who?
Bison—we'll see you
when you get back from
school!

Knock-knock!
 Who's there?
Bless.
 Bless who?
I don't know—I didn't
sneeze.

Knock-Knock!
 Who's there?
Boo!
 Boo who?
Aw, cheer up, it's not that
bad!

Knock-Knock!
Who's there?
Boris!
Boris who?
Boris with another knock-
knock joke!

Knock-knock!

Who's there?
Boysenberry.
Boysenberry who?
Boysenberry cute girls are
all invited to my party.

Knock-knock!
Who's there?
Brad!
Brad who?
Brad dog!
No cookie!

50

Knock-knock!
 Who's there?
Brett!
 Brett who?
Brett you can't guess!

KNOCK-KNOCK!
 Who's there?
Buckle!
 Buckle who?
Buckle get you a
soda pop, but not
much else!

Knock-knock!

Who's there?
Burro!
Burro who?
Burro a cup of sugar from
you?

Knock-knock!
Who's there?
Butternut.
Butternut who?
Butternut try to pick up a
skunk.

Knock-Knock!
 Who's there?
Bunny!
 Bunny who?
Bunny thing is, I know
where the Easter eggs
are!

Knock-Knock!
 Who's there?
Burton!
 Burton who?
Burton me are going
fishing, want to come?

BAP!

Knock-Knock!
 Who's there?
Butter!
 Butter who?
Butter stay inside—
it looks like rain!

C

Knock-knock!
Who's there?
Caesar.
Caesar who?
Caesar great homes for
sharks and dolphins.

Knock-knock!
Who's there?
Cameron.
Cameron who?
Cameron film are all you
need to take photos.

Knock-knock!
Who's there?
Candice.
Candice who?
Candice class get any
more boring?

Knock-knock!
 Who's there?
Candidate.
 Candidate who?
Candidate be changed to
Friday?

Knock-Knock!
 Who's there?
Cannelloni!
 Cannelloni who?
Cannelloni five bucks till next week?

KNOCK-KNOCK!
 Who's there?
Canoe!
 Canoe who?
Canoe please open the door?

Knock-knock!
Who's there?
Canter!
Canter who?
Canter sister come out to
play for a while?

Knock-knock!
 Who's there?
Cantelope!
 Cantelope who?
Cantelope—I'm already married!

Knock-Knock!
 Who's there?
Cargo!
 Cargo who?
Cargo really fast when
you step on the gas!

KNOCK-KNOCK!
 Who's there?
Carmen.
 Carmen who?
Carmen get it!
Dinner's ready!

Knock-Knock!
 Who's there?
Carrie!
 Carrie who?
Carrie this for me, will
you, my back's killing me!

Knock-knock!

Who's there?
Carrot!
Carrot who?
Carrot all about my
opinion?

Knock-knock!
Who's there?
Carson!
Carson who?
Carson the freeway drive
too quickly!

Knock-knock!
 Who's there?
Cash.
 Cash who?
Cashew? That's my
favorite nut.

Knock-knock!
 Who's there?
Cat!
 Cat who?
Cat talk right now; I hab
a cold!

KNOCK-KNOCK!
 Who's there?
Catcher!
 Catcher who?
Catcher before she leaves
here and starts home!

Knock-Knock!
 Who's there?
Catgut!
 Catgut who?
Catgut yer tongue?

Knock-Knock!
  Who's there?
Catsup!
  Catsup who?
Catsup on the roof—want
me to go get him?

Knock-knock!
  Who's there?
Cattle.
  Cattle who?
Cattle always purr when
you pet it.

Knock-knock!
 Who's there?
Cauliflower!
 Cauliflower who?
Cauliflower by another
name and it still smells
as sweet!

Knock-knock!

Who's there?
Cecile.
Cecile who?
Cecile the d-door!
A m-monster's outs-s-side!

KNOCK-KNOCK!

Who's there?
Celeste!
Celeste who?
Celeste time
I'm going to tell you, so
listen up!

Knock-knock!
 Who's there?
Center!
 Center who?
Center a message I was
coming!

Knock-Knock!
Who's there?
Chair!
Chair who?
Chair you go again,
asking silly questions!

Knock-Knock!
Who's there?
Checkmate!
Checkmate who?
Checkmate bounce if
you don't put money in
the bank!

Knock-knock!
Who's there?
Cher.
Cher who?
Cher your toys, and you'll
have lots of friends.

KNOCK-KNOCK!

Who's there?
Chester.
Chester who?
Chester minute,
pardner...you new in this
here town?

Knock-Knock!
  Who's there?
Claire!
  Claire who?
Claire the way, I'm coming through!

Knock-Knock!
Who's there?
Clothesline!
Clothesline who?
Clothesline all over the
floor end up wrinkled!

Knock-Knock!
 Who's there?
Coffin!
 Coffin who?
Coffin that bad means
you got a cold!

KNOCK-KNOCK!

Who's there?
Cole!
Cole who?
Cole me later, I gotta go!

Knock-knock!
 Who's there?
Collar!
 Collar who?
Collar on the phone if you
want to talk to her!

Knock-Knock!
 Who's there?
Colleen!
 Colleen who?
Colleen all cars, Colleen all cars! We have a knock-knock joke in progress!

Knock-Knock!

Who's there?
Cook!
Cook who?
You're the one who's
cuckoo!

Knock-Knock!
 Who's there?
Comb!
 Comb who?
Comb on down and I'll
tell you!

Knock-Knock!

Who's there?
Cows go!
Cows go who?
No, they don't—cows go moo!

Knock-knock!
 Who's there?
Culver.
 Culver who?
Culver up my feet—
they're freezing!

Knock-Knock!
 Who's there?
Cupid!
 Cupid who?
Cupid quiet in there!

D

Knock-knock!
  Who's there?
Dancer!
  Dancer who?
Dancer is de same as de
question!

Knock-knock!
 Who's there?
Dandelion.
 Dandelion who?
Dandelion always growls
at Tony the tiger.

Knock-knock!
 Who's there?
Danielle.
 Danielle who?
Danielle so loud, my ears
hurt.

Knock-Knock!
 Who's there?
Darren!
 Darren who?
Darren you to read
through to the last page
of this knock-knock book!

Knock-knock!
  Who's there?
Daryl.
  Daryl who?
Daryl never be anyone as
weird as you.

Knock-knock!
  Who's there?
Debate.
  Debate who?
Debate is what you use to
catch de fish.

Knock-knock!
  Who's there?
Deceit.
  Deceit who?
Deceit of your jeans has a big hole.

Knock-knock!

Who's there?
Deduct.
Deduct who?
Deduct says, "Quack! Quack!"

Knock-knock!
Who's there?
Denise.
Denise who?
Denise are above de ankles.

Knock-knock!
 Who's there?
Dewey.
 Dewey who?
Dewey really have to go
to school today?

Knock-knock!
 Who's there?
Diego.
 Diego who?
Diego before de B.

Knock-knock!
 Who's there?
Diesel.
 Diesel who?
Diesel teach you to fix
your doorbell.

Knock-knock!
  Who's there?
Dinah snores.
  Dinah snores who?
Dinah snores live in
Jurassic Park.

Knock-Knock!
 Who's there?
Dinosaur!
 Dinosaur who?
Dinosaur, she fell down
playing tennis!

KNOCK-KNOCK!
 Who's there?
Disguise!
 Disguise who?
Disguise killing me with
these knock-knock jokes!

Knock-knock!
 Who's there?
Dishes.
 Dishes who?
Dishes the last time I eat
anchovies for breakfast.

Knock-knock!
 Who's there?
Dish towel.
 Dish towel who?
Dish towel is soaked.
Would you get me a dry
one?

Knock-knock!
Who's there?
Dismay.
Dismay who?
Dismay not be a good
time to knock.

Knock-knock!
 Who's there?
Distress.
 Distress who?
Distress makes me look
like an elephant in a tutu.

Knock-knock!
 Who's there?
Doctor Dolittle.
 Doctor Dolittle who?
Doctor Dolittle to cure my sore throat.

KNOCK KNOCK!
 Who's there?
Don!
 Don who?
Don tell me you don't remember me!

Knock-Knock!
 Who's there?
Don Juan!
 Don Juan who?
Don Juan to go to school
today, let's go to the zoo!

KNOCK-KNOCK!

Who's there?
Doughnut!
Doughnut who?
Doughnut make me
reveal my true identity!
I'm undercover!

Knock-knock!
 Who's there?
Dumbbell!
 Dumbbell who?
Dumbbell doesn't work—
I've been out here forever!

E

Knock-knock!
Who's there?
Eclipse.
Eclipse who?
Eclipse his moustache
when it curls over his
mouth.

Knock-Knock!
Who's there?
Eddy!
Eddy who?
Eddy idea how I can get
rid ub dis cold?

Knock-knock!
 Who's there?
Eel!
 Eel who?
Eel your cold by spending
the day in bed!

Knock-knock!
 Who's there?
Eggs!
 Eggs who?
Eggs it to the left, please,
and no pushing!

Knock-knock!
 Who's there?
Eggshell.
 Eggshell who?
Eggshell be our breakfast
tomorrow morning.

Knock-knock!
Who's there?
Eileen!
Eileen who?
Eileen on your doorbell
for a long time before you
came out!

Knock-knock!

Who's there?
Elaine.
Elaine who?
Elaine down on the couch.
Should I wake him up?

Knock-knock!
 Who's there?
Element!
 Element who?
Element for us to wait
here for her—she said so!

Knock-knock!
 Who's there?
Eliza.
 Eliza who?
Eliza lot, but sometimes
he tells the truth.

KNOCK-KNOCK!

Who's there?

Ellis.

Ellis who?

Ellis the letter that comes before M.

Knock-knock!
 Who's there?
Elvis!
 Elvis who?
Elvis help Santa!

Knock-Knock!
 Who's there?
Emma!
 Emma who?
Emma too early for lunch?

Knock-knock!
  Who's there?
Esau.
  Esau who?
Esau a pit bull and
jumped back on his bike.

Knock-knock!
Who's there?
Esme.
Esme who?
Esme shirt untucked?

Knock-knock!
 Who's there?
Esther!
 Esther who?
Esther bunny!

Knock-knock!
 Who's there?
Stella!
 Stella who?
Stella nother
Esther bunny!

Knock-knock!

Who's there?
Everest!
Everest who?
Everest with those
questions?

Knock-Knock!
Who's there?
Everlast!
Everlast who?
Everlast one
of you better
come out here!

Come out with your
hands up!

Knock-Knock!
Who's there?
Eyeball!
Eyeball who?
Eyeball my eyes out every
time you go!

KNOCK-KNOCK!

Who's there?
Eyedrops.
Eyedrops who?
Eyedrops my keys, then I picks them up.

Knock-knock!
Who's there?
Eyelashes.
Eyelashes who?
Eyelashes myself to the mast during a storm.

F

Knock-Knock!
 Who's there?
Falafel!
 Falafel who?
Falafel my skateboard
and landed on my knee!

Knock-Knock!
 Who's there?
Feline!
 Feline who?
Feline fine,
how about you?

Knock-Knock!

Who's there?
Felix!
Felix who?
Felix me again, I'm not gonna pet your dog anymore!

Knock-Knock!
 Who's there?
Ferris!
 Ferris who?
Ferris fair, you win!

121

Knock-Knock!
 Who's there?
Fiddle!
 Fiddle who?
Fiddle make you happy,
I'll tell you!

Knock-knock!
  Who's there?
Fido!
  Fido who?
Fido what you say, will
you let me in?

Knock-knock!
 Who's there?
Firewood.
 Firewood who?
Firewood sure make
these marshmallows melt
faster.

KNOCK-KNOCK!

 Who's there?
Fish!
 Fish who?
Fish-us temper your dog's
got! He should be on a
leash!

Knock-Knock!
 Who's there?
Fission!
 Fission who?
Fission a bowl are safe
from the cat!

KNOCK-KNOCK!

Who's there?
Flora.
Flora who?
Flora my room
sure is a mess!

Knock-Knock!
Who's there?
Flounder!
Flounder who?
Flounder key on the lawn
—ya want it back?

Knock-Knock!
Who's there?
Francis!
Francis who?
Francis between Spain
and Germany.

Knock-knock!
Who's there?
Freeze!
Freeze who?
Freeze a jolly good fellow!

Knock-knock!
 Who's there?
Frieda.
 Frieda who?
Frieda cow! She's stuck in
the fence!

Knock-Knock!
 Who's there?
Furlong!
 Furlong who?
Furlong time I wanted to
come by and say hi!

Knock-Knock!
 Who's there?
Fuschia!
 Fuschia who?
Fuschia ever call me, I'm
going to be out!

G

Knock-Knock!
 Who's there?
Gabe!
 Gabe who?
Gabe it my best shot and
that's all I can do!

Knock-knock!
 Who's there?
Ghosts go.
 Ghosts go who?
No, silly. Ghosts go "Boo!"

Knock-knock!
 Who's there?
G. I.
 G. I. who?
G. I. wish I had a million
bucks.

Knock-knock!
 Who's there?
Giraffe!
 Giraffe who?
Giraffe 'ter me, I can tell!

Knock-Knock!
Who's there?
Gladys!
Gladys who?
Gladys finally summer
vacation, aren't you?

Knock-knock!
 Who's there?
Glove!
 Glove who?
Glove is all you need!

KNOCK-KNOCK!
 Who's there?
Goblin.
 Goblin who?
Goblin your dinner will
give you a stomachache.

Knock-knock!
 Who's there?
Goliath.
 Goliath who?
Goliath down, you
looketh sleepy.

Knock-knock!
Who's there?
Gopher!
Gopher who?
Gopher the gold and be
happy with the silver—
that's what I say!

KNOCK-KNOCK!

Who's there?
Gorilla!
Gorilla who?
Gorilla cheese is my
favorite for lunch!

Knock-Knock!
 Who's there?
Grape!
 Grape who?
Grape game the other
day, you're still the
champ!

Knock-Knock!
 Who's there?
Greta!
 Greta who?
Greta phone and then I
can stop knocking!

Knock-knock!
 Who's there?
Gruesome.
 Gruesome who?
Gruesome purple
petunias in my garden.

Knock-knock!

Who's there?
Guest.
Guest who?
Guest wrong, now I'll
have to take the math test
again.

Knock-knock!
Who's there?
Gus.
Gus who?
Gus I'll have to come
back later.

Knock-knock!
 Who's there?
Gwen.
 Gwen who?
Gwen fishing? Can I
come?

H

Knock-knock!
 Who's there?
Hairdo.
 Hairdo who?
Hairdo a great job of
keeping your head warm.

Knock-knock!
 Who's there?
Halibut!
 Halibut who?
Halibut you let me in and
we'll talk about it where
it's warm?

Knock-knock!
 Who's there?
Hank!
 Hank who?
Hank you very much!

Knock-knock!
 Who's there?
Hans.
 Hans who?
Hans off my candy bar!

KNOCK-KNOCK!
 Who's there?
Hardy!
 Hardy who?
Hardy a nice way to greet
a friend!

Knock-Knock!
 Who's there?
Hardy!
 Hardy who?
Hardy recognized you
without your glasses!

Knock-knock!
 Who's there?
Harmonica!
 Harmonica who?
Harmonica and her sister
home?

KNOCK-KNOCK!

Who's there?
Harmony.
Harmony who?
Harmony times have I
asked you to open this
door!

Knock-knock!
Who's there?
Harris.
Harris who?
Harris in my eyes, so I'd
better use some gel.

Knock-knock!
 Who's there?
Harry.
 Harry who?
Harry up and answer the door!

KNOCK-KNOCK!
 Who's there?
Hatch-hatch-hatch.
 Hatch-hatch-hatch who?
Bless you! Need a tissue?

Knock-knock!
 Who's there?
Heaven!
 Heaven who?
Heaven we met some-
where before?

KNOCK-KNOCK!

Who's there?
Heidi!
Heidi who?
Heidi Claire, something
smells delicious!

Knock-knock!
 Who's there?
Henrietta.
 Henrietta who?
Henrietta healthy lunch.

KNOCK-KNOCK!
 Who's there?
Hi!
 Hi who?
Hi who, hi who, it's off to
work we go!

Knock-knock!
 Who's there?
Hobbit.
 Hobbit who?
Hobbit your way, smarty-
pants.

Knock-knock!
 Who's there?
Homer.
 Homer who?
Homer away, I always
take a bath on Saturday
night.

Knock-knock!
 Who's there?
Honeycomb.
 Honeycomb who?
Honeycomb your hair
before we go to the dance.

Knock-knock!
 Who's there?
Honeydew.
 Honeydew who?
Honeydew you like your
pizza hot or cold?

Knock-Knock!

Who's there?
House!
House who?
House about you let me
come inside!

Knock-Knock!
Who's there?
Howell!
Howell who?
Howell you ever make
friends if you stay locked
up like that?

Knock-knock!
 Who's there?
Howie!
 Howie who?
Howie forgets who I am
every time, I'll never
know!

Knock-knock!

Who's there?
Hugh!
Hugh who?
Hugh loves ya, baby!

Knock-Knock!
Who's there?
Hugo!
Hugo who?
Hugo on and on about
these knock-knock jokes!

I

Knock-knock!
 Who's there?
Ice cream.
 Ice cream who?
Ice cream when I see
vampires on TV.

Knock-knock!
 Who's there?
Icing.
 Icing who?
Icing a song for you on
your birthday.

Knock-Knock!
 Who's there?
Icy!
 Icy who?
Icy you in there, let me in!

Knock-knock!

Who's there?
Ida.
Ida who?
Ida come earlier, but I
crashed my skateboard.

Knock-knock!
  Who's there?
Iguana!
  Iguana who?
Iguana know where you
heard all these
knock-knock jokes!

KNOCK-KNOCK!
  Who's there?
Imus.
  Imus who?
Imus get out of bed, or I'll
be late for school.

Knock-knock!
 Who's there?
Income.
 Income who?
Income the cats if you
leave the door open.

Knock-knock!
 Who's there?
India!
 India who?
India meantime, why
don't we play some cards!

Knock-knock!
  Who's there?
Intense.
  Intense who?
Intense is where I like to
sleep on camping trips.

Knock-Knock!
  Who's there?
Interrupting cow!
  Interrupting (say
"Mooooooooooooo!" as the
other person is saying
"Interrupting Cow who?")
cow who?

Knock-knock!
 Who's there?
Iona.
 Iona who?
Iona new skateboard,
nyah, nyah.

Knock-knock!
 Who's there?
Iran!
 Iran who?
Iran and ran, but I could
not catch up with you!

Knock-knock!
 Who's there?
Iraq.
 Iraq who?
Iraq my brain for math
test answers.

Knock-knock!
Who's there?
Irene!
Irene who?
Irene you going to invite
me in?

Knock-Knock!
Who's there!
Irish!
Irish who?
Irish you'd take me away
from all this!

Knock-knock!
  Who's there?
Isabel.
  Isabel who?
Isabel out of order?
I had to knock.

Knock-knock!
  Who's there?
Isadore!
  Isadore who?
Isadore locked or can I
just walk in?

KNOCK-KNOCK!
  Who's there?
Isaiah.
  Isaiah who?
Isaiah little prayer before
I go to sleep.

Knock-knock!
 Who's there?
Ishmael!
 Ishmael who?
Ishmael in the mailbox
for you!

Knock-knock!
 Who's there?
Island!
 Island who?
Island my helicopter on
your roof!

Knock-Knock!
 Who's there?
Issue!
 Issue who?
Issue blind? It's me!

KNOCK-KNOCK!

Who's there?
Ivana!
Ivana who?
Ivana come in and watch
the game!

Knock-knock!
Who's there?
Izzy.
Izzy who?
Izzy coming now, or isn't
he?

J

Knock-knock!
Who's there?
Jackal.
Jackal who?
Jackal mow your lawn, if
you pay him.

KNOCK-KNOCK!
Who's there?
Jacket!
Jacket who?
Jacket the mall told me to
come get you!

Knock-Knock!
 Who's there?
Jason!
 Jason who?
Jason your brother will
only get you in trouble!

KNOCK-KNOCK!

Who's there?
Jerome!
Jerome who?
Jerome is so messy, I can't
even see the bed!

Knock-Knock!
  Who's there?
Jerry.
  Jerry who?
Jerry funny, you know
darn well who it is!

Knock-knock!
 Who's there?
Jester.
 Jester who?
Jester minute...I'm fixing
your doorbell.

Knock-knock!
  Who's there?
Jewel!
  Jewel who?
Jewel find out if you open
the door!

Don't make
me pull that
thing down!

Knock-Knock!
  Who's there?
Jimmy!
  Jimmy who?
Jimmy back my book, you
thief!

Knock-Knock!
  Who's there?
Jo!
  Jo who?
Jo, team, Jo!

KNOCK-KNOCK!
  Who's there?
Joey!
  Joey who?
Joey to the world!
It's Christmas!

Knock-Knock!
  Who's there?
Juan!
  Juan who?
Juan to go
for a pizza?

Knock-knock!
  Who's there?
Juanita.
  Juanita who?
Juanita chocolate-covered
ant?

Knock-knock!
 Who's there?
Juicy.
 Juicy who?
Juicy any ghosts under
my bed?

Knock-Knock!
 Who's there?
Julius!
 Julius who?
Julius just jealous that
you know all the good
jokes!

Knock-knock!
 Who's there?
Juno.
 Juno who?
Juno what time it is now?

Knock-knock!
 Who's there?
Justice.
 Justice who?
Justice I thought...your doorbell's broken.

Knock-knock!
 Who's there?
Justin.
 Justin who?
Justin the neighborhood
and thought I'd say hello.

KNOCK-KNOCK!
 Who's there?
Justina.
 Justina who?
Justina nick of time,
I caught my pet
tarantula before
it escaped.

K

Knock-knock!
  Who's there?
Kanga.
  Kanga who?
Not kangawho, silly—
kangaroo!

Knock-knock!
 Who's there?
Katmandu.
 Katmandu who?
Katmandu exactly what
Catwoman do.

Knock-knock!
 Who's there?
Keith.
 Keith who?
Keith me, thweetheart.

Knock-knock!
  Who's there?
Kenny!
  Kenny who?
Kenny come out or can't he?

Knock-knock!

Who's there?
Kent.
Kent who?
Kent go with you, I'm grounded.

Knock-Knock!
 Who's there?
Kenya.
 Kenya who?
Kenya fix the doorbell—
I've been knocking for
hours!

Knock-Knock!
 Who's there?
Kerry!
 Kerry who?
Kerry me upstairs, would
you? I'm pooped!

Knock-knock!

Who's there?
Ketchup!
Ketchup who?
Ketchup before you get
left behind!

Knock-knock!
Who's there?
Kiefer.
Kiefer who?
Kiefer my door is lost.

Knock-knock!
  Who's there?
Kimmy.
  Kimmy who?
Kimmy a little kiss,
Sweetie.

Knock-knock!
  Who's there?
Kip.
  Kip who?
Kip your sneaky hands
out of my popcorn!

KNOCK-KNOCK!

Who's there?
Kitty litter.
Kitty litter who?
Kitty litter mouse
get away!

Knock-Knock!
Who's there?
Klaus!
Klaus who?
Klaus the window, I can
hear your television all
the way down the street!

Knock-knock!
 Who's there?
Knotty.
 Knotty who?
Knotty little kids get time out.

Knock-Knock!
 Who's there?
Kumquat!
 Kumquat who?
Kumquat may, we'll
always be friends!

L

Knock-knock!
 Who's there?
Lady.
 Lady who?
Lady mat on the porch
and I won't track mud in
the house.

KNOCK-KNOCK!

 Who's there?
Landon.
 Landon who?
Landon on your belly
hurts!

Knock-knock!
 Who's there?
Leda.
 Leda who?
Leda horse to water but you can't make him drink.

Knock-knock!
 Who's there?
Lego!
 Lego who?
Lego of the door and I'll tell you!

Knock-Knock!

Who's there?
Leif!
Leif who?
Leif me alone with all
your silly questions!

Knock-Knock!
Who's there?
Lena!
Lena who?
Lena little closer and
maybe I'll tell you!

Knock-knock!
 Who's there?
Lettuce and turnips.
 Lettuce and turnips who?
Lettuce see if any evi-
dence turnips before we
call the cops.

Knock-Knock!
 Who's there?
Lettuce!
 Lettuce who?
Lettuce in or we'll huff
and we'll puff and we'll
blow the house down!

KNOCK-KNOCK!

 Who's there?
Linda.
 Linda who?
Linda hand, please—
I can't seem to open
this door!

Knock-Knock!
  Who's there?
Lion!
  Lion who?
Lion down on the job will
get you fired!

Knock-knock!
 Who's there?
Lionel!
 Lionel who?
Lionel only get you into
trouble!

Knock-knock!
  Who's there?
Lipstick.
  Lipstick who?
Lipstick together when
you blow bubble gum.

Knock-knock!
  Who's there?
Lisa!
  Lisa who?
Lisa know who my friends
are!

Knock-knock!
 Who's there?
Liver!
 Liver who?
Liver die, it's up to you!

Knock-knock!
 Who's there?
Lizard!
 Lizard who?
Lizard you were having a party and she invited me!

Knock-knock!
 Who's there?
Luke.
 Luke who?
Luke through the keyhole and you might find out.

Knock-knock!
 Who's there?
Luther.
 Luther who?
Luther jeans would fit me
much better.

M

Knock-Knock!
 Who's there?
Mabel!
 Mabel who?
Mabel syrup is great on waffles!

Knock-knock!
 Who's there?
Macaw.
 Macaw who?
Macaw won't start. Can you give me a lift?

Knock-knock!
 Who's there?
Manatee!
 Manatee who?
Manatee would really
warm me up right now!

Knock-knock!
 Who's there?
Mandy.
 Mandy who?
Mandy lifeboats—we've
hit an iceberg!

213

Knock-Knock!
Who's there?
Manny!
Manny who?
Manny people ask me
that question. I wonder
why?

Knock-Knock!
Who's there?
Marcus!
Marcus who?
Marcus down for two
tickets, we're going to
the show!

Knock-Knock!

Who's there?
Maria!
Maria who?
Maria me, I love you!

Knock-knock!
 Who's there?
Martian!
 Martian who?
Martian all day is only
going to make your feet
hurt!

216

Knock-knock!
 Who's there?
Mascot!
 Mascot who?
Mascot a cold. You don't have it, do you?

Knock-Knock!
 Who's there?
Matthew!
 Matthew who?
Matthew need help with. Science you might be better at!

Knock-knock!
 Who's there?
Maura.
 Maura who?
Maura those French fries
and another burger, please.

Knock-knock!
 Who's there?
Maya.
 Maya who?
Maya good joke teller?

Knock-knock!
 Who's there?
Meat patty.
 Meat patty who?
Meat Patty, then meet her
brother Frank Furter.

Knock-knock!
 Who's there?
Meteor!
 Meteor who?
Meteor new neighbor!

Knock-knock!
 Who's there?
Mia.
 Mia who?
Mia genius;
you a
dummy.

Knock-Knock!
Who's there?
Mice!
Mice who?
Mice to make your
acquaintance!

Knock-knock!
Who's there?
Midas!
Midas who?
Midas well admit it,
you don't even know who
I am!

Knock-Knock!
 Who's there?
Mission!
 Mission who?
Mission you is
making me sad,
come home!

Knock-knock!
 Who's there?
Missouri!
 Missouri who?
Missouri loves company!

KNOCK-KNOCK!

Who's there?
Mistake!
Mistake who?
Mistake aspirin if you
have a headache!

Knock-knock!
Who's there?
Mister!
Mister who?
Mister birthday party but
I got something for her!

Knock-Knock!
Who's there?
Modem!
Modem who?
Modem lawns, the grass
is getting long!

224

KNOCK-KNOCK!

Who's there?
Morrie!
Morrie who?
Morrie talks, the sleepier
I get!

Knock-Knock!
Who's there?
Moustache!
Moustache who?
Moustache you a
question, you ready?

Knock-knock!
 Who's there?
Musket.
 Musket who?
Musket a job—I'm broke.

Knock-knock!
 Who's there?
Myth.
 Myth who?
Myth my two fwont teefth
in my mowfth.

N

Knock-knock!
Who's there?
Nadia.
Nadia who?
Nadia head if you under-
stand the question.

Knock-knock!
 Who's there?
Nanny.
 Nanny who?
Nanny one going to
answer this door?

KNOCK-KNOCK!
 Who's there?
Nantucket.
 Nantucket who?
Nantucket, but she'll give
it right back.

Knock-knock!
 Who's there?
Needle.
 Needle who?
Needle little sympathy.

Knock-knock!
 Who's there?
Nickel.
 Nickel who?
Nickel dance the hula if
we buy him a grass skirt.

Knock-knock!

Who's there?
Noah.
Noah who?
Noah good place to find
more jokes?

Knock-knock!
Who's there?
Norma Lee.
Norma Lee who?
Norma Lee I rinse my
mouth after the dog
kisses me.

Knock-knock!

Who's there?
Norway.
Norway who?
Norway am I going to
open this door.

O

Knock-knock!
  Who's there?
Oil.
  Oil who?
Oil see you later, alligator.

Knock-knock!
Who's there?
Olive!
Olive who?
Olive my other friends
know who I am!

Knock-knock!
 Who's there?
Oliver.
 Oliver who?
Oliver clothes got wet
when she fell into
the pool.

Knock-Knock!
 Who's there?
Ollie!
 Ollie who?
Ollie want is to come
inside.

Knock-knock!
 Who's there?
Omelet and butter.
 Omelet and butter who?
Omelet stronger than I
look, so you butter
watch out.

Knock-Knock!
 Who's there?
Orange!
 Orange who?
Orange you gonna let
me in?

KNOCK-KNOCK!
 Who's there?
Orange juice!
 Orange juice who?
Orange juice the guy I
just talked to?

Knock-knock!
 Who's there?
Osborn.
 Osborn who?
Osborn in a hospital.
Where's you born?

Knock-knock!
 Who's there?
Ostrich!
 Ostrich who?
Ostrich and
ostrich,
but I'm still
stiff!

KNOCK-KNOCK!

Who's there?
Oswald!
Oswald who?
Oswald my ice cream so quickly, my head hurts!

Knock-Knock!
Who's there?
Otto!
Otto who?
Otto be asleep by now!

Knock-knock!
 Who's there?
Owl!
 Owl who?
Owl be seeing you!

Knock-knock!
 Who's there?
Ozzie.
 Ozzie who?
Ozzie you when
you get back.

P

Knock-knock!
 Who's there?
Panther.
 Panther who?
Panther no panth, I'm
going thwimming.

Knock-knock!
 Who's there?
Parka!
 Parka who?
Parka cross the street is
open—let's go!

Knock-Knock!

Who's there?
Paris!
Paris who?
Paris good but apple is better!

Knock-knock!
Who's there?
Pasta!
Pasta who?
Pasta cheese, please!

Knock-knock!
 Who's there?
Pecan.
 Pecan who?
Pecan somebody your
own size!

KNOCK-KNOCK!
 Who's there?
Peeka.
 Peeka who?
Not peeka who, silly...
peekaboo.

Knock-Knock!

Who's there?
Philip!
Philip who?
Philip my gas tank, will you?

Knock-knock!
 Who's there?
Phyllis.
 Phyllis who?
Phyllis in on the latest
gossip.

Knock-Knock!
 Who's there?
Pickle!
 Pickle who?
Pickle little flower and
give it to your mother!

Knock-Knock!
Who's there?
Pigment!
Pigment who?
Pigment a lot to me, have
you seen him?

Knock-Knock!
 Who's there?
Pinafore.
 Pinafore who?
Pinafore your thoughts!

Knock-knock!

Who's there?
Pizza.
Pizza who?
Pizza nice guy when you
get to know him.

Knock-Knock!
Who's there?
Plane!
Plane who?
Plane dumb won't help
you now!

Knock-knock!
 Who's there?
Plato.
 Plato who?
Plato nachos, please.

Knock-Knock!
 Who's there?
Police!
 Police who?
Police let
me in, it's
cold out
here!

Hey, It's cold out here!

KNOCK-KNOCK!

Who's there?
Poodle.
Poodle who?
Poodle little chow in
Fido's dish, will you?

Knock-Knock!
Who's there?
Porpoise!
Porpoise who?
Porpoise of my visit is an
unpaid bill!

Knock-knock!

Who's there?
Poster!
Poster who?
Poster remember your
friends' names!

Knock-knock!
Who's there?
Pressure!
Pressure who?
Pressure face up against
the glass and you'll be
able to tell!

Knock-knock!
 Who's there?
Pudding.
 Pudding who?
Pudding your hand in a
crocodile's mouth is
really dumb.

KNOCK-KNOCK!

 Who's there?
Punch.
 Punch who?
Not me!

Knock-knock!

Who's there?
Pup!
Pup who?
Pup goes the weasel—
that's who!

Knock-Knock!
Who's there?
Pylon!
Pylon who?
Pylon the knock-knocks,
I love 'em!

Q

Knock-knock!
 Who's there?
Q-T.
 Q-T who?
Q-T pie, you're adorable.

Knock-knock!
 Who's there?
Quacker.
 Quacker who?
Quacker cwumbs are in
my bed.

Knock-knock!

Who's there?
Queen.
Queen who?
Queen up your room,
please.

Knock-knock!
Who's there?
Queue.
Queue who?
Queue better floss that
spinach out of your teeth.

R

Knock-knock!
 Who's there?
Rabbit!
 Rabbit who?
Rabbit up—
I'll take it!

Knock-knock!
 Who's there?
Radio!
 Radio who?
Radio not, here I come!

Knock-knock!
 Who's there?
Raisin.
 Raisin who?
Raisin chickens is a
cheep-cheep job.

Knock-knock
 Who's there?
Raptor!
 Raptor who?
Raptor arms around me—
she loves me!

Knock-Knock!
 Who's there?
Ray!
 Ray who?
Ray-member me?

Knock-knock!
Who's there?
Razor.
Razor who?
Razor hand if you have
the correct answer.

Knock-knock!
 Who's there?
Reindeer!
 Reindeer who?
Reindeer. Looks like we'll
have to have the picnic
another day!

KNOCK-KNOCK!

 Who's there?
Ringo.
 Ringo who?
Ringo on the bride's
finger.

Knock-Knock!
  Who's there?
Riot!
  Riot who?
Riot on time, here I am!

Knock-Knock!
  Who's there?
Robin!
  Robin who?
Robin the bank will get
you in jail!

Knock-knock!

Who's there?
Rocky!
Rocky who?
Rocky bye baby on the treetop!

Knock-Knock!
Who's there?
Romeo.
Romeo who?
Romeo-ver to the other side of the river, would ya?

Knock-knock!
  Who's there?
Ron.
  Ron who?
Ron faster! There's a
tyrannosaurus after us!

KNOCK-KNOCK!

Who's there?
Rufus!
Rufus who?
Rufus falling in!

Knock-Knock!
Who's there?
Russell.
Russell who?
Russell me up some grub
and I'll tell ya.

Knock-knock!
 Who's there?
Russian!
 Russian who?
Russian around all day
makes me tired!

S

Knock-knock!
 Who's there?
Saddle!
 Saddle who?
Saddle I have to miss
your party!

Knock-knock!
 Who's there?
Sadie.
 Sadie who?
Sadie magic word, and I'll
pass the nuts.

Knock-Knock!
Who's there?
Salmon!
Salmon who?
Salmon chanted evening,
you may meet a stranger!

KNOCK-KNOCK!
Who's there?
Samoa.
Samoa who?
Samoa that super-sized
soda will give me the
hiccups.

Knock-knock!
  Who's there?
Sandal!
  Sandal who?
Sandal over my feet—
that's the beach!

Knock-knock!
 Who's there?
Santa.
 Santa who?
Santa e-mail to you but
you never replied.

KNOCK-KNOCK!
 Who's there?
Sarah!
 Sarah who?
Sarah nother way we
could do this?

Knock-knock!
 Who's there?
Satellite!
 Satellite who?
Satellite on in your
window?

Knock-knock!
 Who's there?
Say!
 Say who?
Who!

KNOCK-KNOCK!

Who's there?
Scott!
Scott who?
Scott to be some kind of
way out of here!

Knock-knock!
Who's there?
Selma.
Selma who?
Selma bike, then I'll buy
a scooter.

Knock-knock!

Who's there?
Senior.
Senior who?
Senior boa constrictor
around here lately?

Knock-knock!
Who's there?
Sharon!
Sharon who?
Sharon with people is
how you make friends!

Knock-Knock!
 Who's there?
Sheep!
 Sheep who?
Sheep-ritty, don't you
think?

Knock-knock!
 Who's there?
Sheila!
 Sheila who?
Sheila only break your
heart, my friend!

KNOCK-KNOCK!
 Who's there?
Shelby!
 Shelby who?
Shelby be sad she missed
you!

Knock-knock!
Who's there?
Shellfish!
Shellfish who?
Shellfish of you to forget
my name!

Knock-knock!
 Who's there?
Sherbet!
 Sherbet who?
Sherbet this'll be a great
evening!

Knock-knock!
  Who's there?
Sherwood!
  Sherwood who?
Sherwood like to come in
and visit!

Knock-knock!
  Who's there?
Shirley!
  Shirley who?
Shirley you can't have for-
gotten my name already!

Knock-knock!
 Who's there?
Shortstop!
 Shortstop who?
Shortstop you from
getting too hot in the
summer!

Knock-Knock!
 Who's there?
Shower!
 Shower who?
Shower you care and
send flowers!

KNOCK-KNOCK!
 Who's there?
Sid.
 Sid who?
Sid down and speak up.

Knock-Knock!
 Who's there?
Sinker!
 Sinker who?
Sinker swim, it's up to
you!

KNOCK-KNOCK!

Who's there?
Ski tow.
Ski tow who?
Ski tow bites itch like
crazy.

Knock-knock!
 Who's there?
Snot!
 Snot who?
Snot my fault!

Knock-Knock!
 Who's there?
Snow!
 Snow who?
Snow way I'm waiting out here—it's freezing!

Knock-knock!
 Who's there?
Soda!
 Soda who?
Soda first thing you have
to do is to remember my
name!

Knock-Knock!
 Who's there?
Soldier!
 Soldier who?
Soldier comics yet?

Knock-Knock!
 Who's there?
Sonata!
 Sonata who?
Sonata-s bad as every-
body says!

Knock-knock!
 Who's there?
Sonia.
 Sonia who?
Sonia matter of time
before I turn into a
werewolf.

Knock-Knock!
 Who's there?
Soup!
 Soup who?
Soup-erman to the rescue!

Knock-Knock!

Who's there?
Sparkle!
Sparkle who?
Sparkle start a fire if
you're not careful!

Knock-Knock!
Who's there?
Sparrow!
Sparrow who?
Sparrow little change, pal?

Knock-knock!
 Who's there?
Spell.
 Spell who?
W-H-O.

Knock-Knock!
 Who's there?
Stan!
 Stan who?
Stan back—I'm breaking
the door down!

Knock-Knock!
Who's there?
Sunday!
Sunday who?
Sunday in the future we'll meet in person!

Knock-Knock!
 Who's there?
Stork!
 Stork who?
Stork up on supplies—
I'm staying a while!

Knock-Knock!
 Who's there?
Stubborn!
 Stubborn who?
Stubborn your toe sure
hurts! Ow!

Knock-Knock!
 Who's there?
Sturdy!
 Sturdy who?
Sturdy pot, de soup is
burning!

KNOCK-KNOCK!

Who's there?
Suture!
Suture who?
Suture self—be that way
if you want to!

Knock-Knock!
Who's there?
Sweden!
Sweden who?
Sweden sour chicken!

T

Knock-knock!
 Who's there?
Talia.
 Talia who?
Talia a bedtime story if
you put your jammies on.

Knock-knock!
 Who's there?
Tanks!
 Tanks who?
Tanks for asking!

Knock-knock!
 Who's there?
Tara.
 Tara who?
Tara hole in your T-shirt?

Knock-knock!
 Who's there?
Tarzan.
 Tarzan who?
Tarzan stripes decorate
flags of many nations.

Knock-knock!
 Who's there?
Teacher!
 Teacher who?
Teacher my
name, would
you!

Knock-Knock!
Who's there?
Termite!
Termite who?
Termite be something
wrong with your glasses!

Knock-knock!
  Who's there?
Terrace!
  Terrace who?
Terrace a spider on my
shoulder—get it off!

Knock-Knock!
  Who's there?
Tex!
  Tex who?
Tex one to know one!

Knock-knock!
Who's there?
Thirsty!
Thirsty who?
Thirsty makes me knock,
then he forgets my name!

KNOCK-KNOCK!
Who's there?
Thistle!
Thistle who?
Thistle be the last time I
visit you! Sheesh!

Knock-knock!
 Who's there?
Thomas!
 Thomas who?
Thomas
something
to tell you!

Knock-knock!
 Who's there?
Throat.
 Throat who?
Throat to me, and I'll
score a touchdown.

Knock-knock!

Who's there?
Thumb.
Thumb who?
Thumb like it hot, thumb
like it cold.

Knock-knock!
Who's there?
Thumping!
Thumping who?
Thumping tells me this
isn't your first knock-
knock joke!

KNOCK-KNOCK!

Who's there?
Tidal!
Tidal who?
Tidal the shoelaces
together—this is going to
be hilarious!

Knock-knock!
 Who's there?
Tilda.
 Tilda who?
Tilda sun rises, I'll be
doing my homework.

Knock-knock!

 Who's there?
Tom Sawyer.
 Tom Sawyer who?
Tom Sawyer underwear
in gym class.

Knock-knock!
 Who's there?
Toucan!
 Toucan who?
Toucan play at this game,
my friend!

Knock-knock!
 Who's there?
Treble!
 Treble who?
Treble with you is, you
never remember anything!

Knock-knock!

Who's there?
Tuba.
Tuba who?
Tuba toothpaste makes
my teeth sparkle.

Knock-knock!
Who's there?
Tulips.
Tulips who?
Tulips kiss better than
one lip.

Knock-Knock!
 Who's there?
Tuna!
 Tuna who?
Tuna piano and it sounds better!

Knock-knock!

Who's there?
Tunis!
Tunis who?
Tunis stuck in my head—
can you hear it too?

Knock-Knock!
Who's there?
Turnip!
Turnip who?
Turnip the volume—
I can't hear the music!

Knock-Knock!
 Who's there?
Tyson!
 Tyson who?
Tyson garlic around your neck. It's the vampire!

U

Knock-knock!
 Who's there?
U-2.
 U-2 who?
U-2 can be a
rock star in
ten easy
lessons!

Knock-Knock!
 Who's there?
Udder!
 Udder who?
Udder foolishness to keep
reading these jokes!

Knock-knock!
 Who's there?
Uganda.
 Uganda who?
Uganda lot of
weight over vacation.

Knock-knock!
 Who's there?
Unaware.
 Unaware who?
Unaware sticking out of
your jeans!

Knock-knock!
Who's there?
Unit.
Unit who?
Unit me a sweater, and I'll
knit you some mittens.

Knock-Knock!
Who's there?
Uphill!
Uphill who?
Uphill could take your
headache away!

Knock-knock!
 Who's there?
Uruguay.
 Uruguay who?
Uruguay who knows how
to treat a gwirl.

Knock-knock!
 Who's there?
Usher.
 Usher who?
Usher up...
she's singing
too loud.

V

Knock-knock!
 Who's there?
Vanessa.
 Vanessa who?
Vanessa bus coming?

Knock-Knock!
 Who's there?
Vaughn!
 Vaughn who?
Vaughn day you'll stop
acting so crazy!

Knock-knock!

Who's there?
Venice!
Venice who?
Venice the party going to start?

315

Knock-knock!
 Who's there?
Vera.
 Vera who?
Vera interesting...can you
repeat that?

KNOCK-KNOCK!
 Who's there?
Violins!
 Violins who?
Violins is a bad way to
settle an argument.

Knock-knock!

Who's there?

Viper!

Viper who?

Viper feet before you walk inside the house!

Knock-knock!

Who's there?

Voodoo.

Voodoo who?

Voodoo you think you're kidding?

W

Knock-knock!
 Who's there?
W.
 W who?
W, and your clone can
answer the door!

Knock-knock!
 Who's there?
Waddle.
 Waddle who?
Waddle you do if I knock
again?

Knock-Knock!
  Who's there?
Walnut!
  Walnut who?
Walnut too sturdy, don't
lean on it!

KNOCK-KNOCK!

Who's there?
Wanda!
Wanda who?
Wanda what you're doing
in there!

Knock-Knock!
Who's there?
Water!
Water who?
Water you waiting for?
Open up!

Knock-knock!
 Who's there?
Watson!
 Watson who?
Watson the agenda for
tonight?

Knock-Knock!
 Who's there?
Wayne!
 Wayne who?
Wayne, wayne go away!
Come again some
other day!

Knock-Knock!
 Who's there?
Weaken!
 Weaken who?
Weaken still be friends!

Knock-knock!
  Who's there?
Wendy.
  Wendy who?
Wendy moon comes up,
de sun goes down.

Knock-knock!
  Who's there?
Wes.
  Wes who?
Wes the exit? I'm lost!

KNOCK-KNOCK!
  Who's there?
Whale!
  Whale who?
Whale never get there if
you just stand around
asking questions!

Knock-Knock!
 Who's there?
Whenever!
 Whenever who?
Whenever body going to
stop asking me that?

Knock-knock!
 Who's there?
Who?
 Who who?
What are you, an owl?

Knock-knock!

Who's there?
Why do owls go.
Why do owls go who?
Because that's how they
talk, silly!

Knock-knock!
Who's there?
Wiggle.
Wiggle who?
Wiggle fall off your head
if the wind blows hard.

Knock-Knock!
 Who's there?
Wigwam!
 Wigwam who?
Wigwam your head when
it's cold!

KNOCK-KNOCK!

Who's there?
William!
William who?
William make me a
sandwich?

Knock-Knock!
Who's there?
Willow!
Willow who?
Willow quit it with the
knock-knocks already?

Knock-Knock!
 Who's there?
Willy!
 Willy who?
Willy let
me on
the team
or not?

Knock-Knock!
 Who's there?
Window!
 Window who?
Window we leave for
school?

KNOCK-KNOCK!

Who's there?
Wire.
Wire who?
Wire you asking? It's me,
knucklehead.

Knock-knock!
Who's there?
Witches.
Witches who?
Witches the one you
want? This one or that?

Knock-knock!

Who's there?
Wooden shoe.
Wooden shoe who?
Wooden shoe like to sleep over?

Knock-knock!
Who's there?
Woody!
Woody who?
Woody stop with all the knock-knocks!

Knock-knock!
Who's there?
Wonton.
Wonton who?
Wonton more pizza than you can eat is a waste of food.

KNOCK-KNOCK!

Who's there?
Woodchuck.
Woodchuck who?
Woodchuck mow the lawn
if we paid him?

X

Knock-knock!
Who's there?
X.
X who?
X and bacon are my
favorite breakfast foods.

Knock-knock!
Who's there?
XL.
XL who?
XL at sports and you'll be
famous.

KNOCK-KNOCK!

Who's there?
Xerox.
Xerox who?
Xerox fell on my head
when I went mountain
climbing.

y

Knock-Knock!
 Who's there?
Yam!
 Yam who?
Yam what I am!

Knock-knock!
 Who's there?
Yaw.
 Yaw who?
Giddyap! Ride 'em,
cowboy!

Knock-Knock!

Who's there?
Yoda!
Yoda who?
Yoda one who wants to know, so why don't you guess!

Knock-knock!
Who's there?
Yolanda.
Yolanda who?
Yolanda plane on the runway.

Knock-knock!
 Who's there?
Yoo.
 Yoo who?
Yoo-hoo,
yourself.

Knock-Knock!
 Who's there?
Yugo!
 Yugo who?
Yugo first, I'll be right
behind ya!

Knock-knock!

Who's there?

Yuma.

Yuma who?

Yuma very best friend.

Knock-knock!

Who's there?

Yukon.

Yukon who?

Yukon come with us if you pay your share.

Knock-knock!
 Who's there?
Yule.
 Yule who?
Yule be sorry
if you miss
Santa.

Knock-Knock!
 Who's there?
Yuri!
 Yuri who?
Yuri up and open the
door!

Knock-knock!
 Who's there?
Yvonne.
 Yvonne who?
Yvonne my own mother
doesn't recognize me with
this wig on.

Z

Knock-Knock!
 Who's there?
Zany!
 Zany who?
Zany way to get you to
stop with the knock-
knocks?

Knock-knock!
 Who's there?
Zeno.
 Zeno who?
Zeno evil, hear no evil,
speak no evil.

Knock-knock!
 Who's there?
Zeus.
 Zeus who?
Zeus are where wild
animals are caged.

Knock-knock!
 Who's there?
Zing.
 Zing who?
Zing zome zongs with me,
okay?

KNOCK-KNOCK!

 Who's there?
Zoe!
 Zoe who?
Zoe doesn't recognize my
voice now?

KNOCK-KNOCK!

 Who's there?
Zoom.
 Zoom who?
Zoom did you expect?

Knock-knock!
 Who's there?
Zounds.
 Zounds who?
Zounds! Zounds like this
might be the last joke.
It is!

Index